It's Easy To Play Tchaikovsky.

Wise Publications
London/New York/Sydney

Exclusive Distributors:
Music Sales Limited
8/9 Frith Street, London W1V 5TZ, England.
Music Sales Pty Limited
120 Rothschild Avenue, Rosebery, NSW 2018, Australia.

This book © Copyright 1991 by Wise Publications.
Order No. AM82926 ISBN 0.7119.2494.5

Art direction by Michael Bell Design.
Cover illustration by Paul Leith.
Arranged by Barry Todd.
Music processed by Musicprint.
Typeset by Capital Setters.

Music Sales' complete catalogue lists thousands of
titles and is free from your local music shop,
or direct from Music Sales Limited.
Please send eight first class stamps for postage to
Music Sales Limited, 8/9 Frith Street, London W1V 5TZ.

Your Guarantee of Quality:

As publishers, we strive to produce every book to
the highest commercial standards.

All the music has been freshly engraved, and the
book has been carefully designed to minimise awkward page turns,
and to make playing from it a real pleasure.

Particular care has been given to specifying acid-free,
neutral-sized paper which has not been chlorine bleached but produced
with special regard for the environment.
Throughout, the printing and binding have been planned to ensure a sturdy,
attractive publication which should give years of enjoyment.

If your copy fails to meet our high standards, please inform us
and we will gladly replace it.

Printed in the United Kingdom by
Caligraving Limited, Thetford, Norfolk.

Piano Concerto No.1

in B flat minor, Op.23 (First Movement)

Composed by Peter Ilich Tchaikovsky

1812 Overture

Op.49

Composed by Peter Ilich Tchaikovsky

Allegro vivace

March from The Nutcracker Suite

Op.71

Composed by Peter Ilich Tchaikovsky

Tempo di marcia

Waltz from Swan Lake

Op.20

Composed by Peter Ilich Tchaikovsky

Tempo di valse

Symphony No.6

in B minor, Op.74 'Pathétique' (First Movement)

Composed by Peter Ilich Tchaikovsky

Dance Of The Sugar Plum Fairy

from The Nutcracker Suite, Op.71

Composed by Peter Ilich Tchaikovsky

Romeo And Juliet

Fantasy Overture in B minor

Composed by Peter Ilich Tchaikovsky

Waltz from Symphony No.5

in E minor, Op.64

Composed by Peter Ilich Tchaikovsky

Allegro moderato

Danse Des Mirlitons

from The Nutcracker Suite, Op.71

Composed by Peter Ilich Tchaikovsky

Slavonic March

in B flat, Op.31

Composed by Peter Ilich Tchaikovsky

Waltz from Serenade For Strings

Op.48

Composed by Peter Ilich Tchaikovsky

Scene from Swan Lake

Op.20

Composed by Peter Ilich Tchaikovsky

Waltz Of The Flowers

from The Nutcracker Suite, Op.71

Composed by Peter Ilich Tchaikovsky

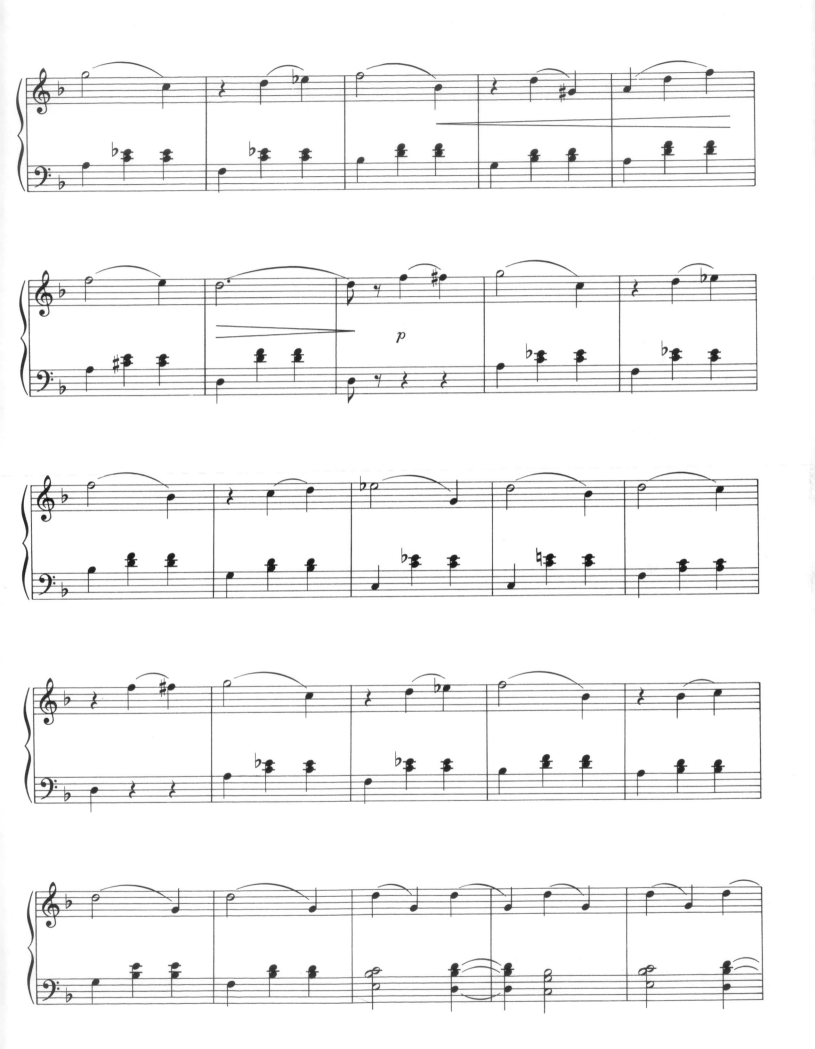

Symphony No.5
in E minor, Op.64 (Second Movement)

Composed by Peter Ilich Tchaikovsky

Andante cantabile